Donkeys Can't Sleep in Bathtubs
and other crazy laws

by
Susan Dach

illustrated by
Patrick M. Reynolds

Watermill Press

ACKNOWLEDGMENTS

I wish to give special thanks to my illustrator, Patrick M. Reynolds; to my agent, Richard Huttner; to my cousin, Jill Silberberg; and to all my friends who helped me with this book.

3

INTRODUCTION

All the laws in this book are real. But they are not all enforced. Even so, they sure are a lot of fun to read. When you know the stories behind them, the laws are sometimes even more entertaining.

For instance, one of the laws in the book is:

In New York State, you have to have a license to hang a clothesline in your front yard.

How did this law come to be?

5

In 1956, a Mr. and Mrs. Stover placed a clothesline in the front yard of their home. They filled it with old clothes and rags. They did this because they felt city taxes were too high. It was a protest. During each of the next five years, they added another clothesline, this time hanging old uniforms, underwear, and even a scarecrow.

The city fathers were upset. They did not like the Stovers' way of showing that high taxes were making them poor. So the city fathers passed a law forbidding clotheslines in front yards unless you had a permit. Mr. and Mrs. Stover applied for one. Do you think they got it?

No, they were refused. They kept their clotheslines up anyway, and they were hauled into court. You may think the Stovers should have won their case.

The Judge said the city had a right to keep the Stovers' neighborhood looking tidy. The clotheslines had to go, and Mr. and Mrs. Stover had to put their old clothes back in the attic.

I wish I could tell you more about all the zany laws in this book. But there is not the space. You will just have to enjoy reading them. Happily, there is no law against laughing.

In the city limits of Mount Dora, Florida, a pet rooster cannot say cock-a-doodle-do.

On Sunday, you are not allowed to auction off a turtle in Kansas City, Missouri.

In Lehigh, Nebraska, it is against the law to sell doughnut holes.

Uncle Sam says *No!* to taking a picture of a dollar bill or of a postage stamp.

In New York, you can teach your pet parrot to *speak* but not to *squawk*.

To sell song books on the streets of Richmond, Virginia, you must buy a license for 93¢.

Shellfish may not be sold from pushcarts in New York City.

No women can play Santa Claus in Minnesota.

If your dog chases a goat or a sheep in Memphis, you can be fined $25.

In Washington, D.C., you can be put in jail if you are cruel to animals.

In Centerville, Ohio, cars are not allowed to scare horses.

If a horse keels over in New York City, you should put a lantern next to his head.

No signs can be put on telephone poles in Texarkana, Texas.

Don't go tadpole hunting in Pennsylvania on Sundays. It's against the law.

In Illinois, if you want to park, you can't bump someone else's car to make room for your own.

A 1930's law on St. Thomas in the Virgin Islands forbids riding on the running board of an automobile.

A policeman can stop people from marching down the street in Tacoma, Washington.

If you want to hold a costume ball in New York City, you have to ask the Mayor's permission.

In Connecticut, kids cannot
charm bees away from a bee
keeper.

In Los Altos Hills, California, two or more joggers running together need a permit from the police.

In New York State, you have to have a license to hang a clothesline in your front yard.

If you snore so loudly you wake up your neighbor in Dunn, North Carolina, you are in trouble with the law.

Pet goldfish that make a
disturbance are not allowed
to ride buses in Seattle.

You may not play pinball in Athens, Georgia.

In New York, a parent cannot allow his child to be a boxer or a wrestler — or even a rag-picker!

Did you know in Spokane, Washington, you can't buy a television on Sunday, but you can buy a radio?

The US Government makes it a crime to give false weather reports.

In Dover, North Carolina, you can be arrested for keeping pigs outside your kitchen window.

In New Jersey, you have to stop your car if a horse passes close by.

In Maine, dentists cannot advertise that they sell false teeth.

Vendors are not supposed to sell peanuts or candy in California parks.

In downtown Los Angeles, it is a *no-no* for anybody to ride on the roof of a car.

Air at gas stations in Hempstead, Long Island, has to be free.

You cannot eat garlic and go straight to the theatre in Gary, Indiana.

In Oklahoma, you may not take a bite of another person's hamburger.

In Mississippi, the state librarian has to be a woman.

If you bother a butterfly in Pacific Grove, California, you can be fined $500.

Winona Lake, Indiana restaurants are not supposed to serve ice cream cones on Sunday.

If you see a horse on a Detroit street, don't throw a banana peel in front of him. It's against the law.

It is against the law to disturb a bullfrog or cottontail rabbit in Hayden, Arizona.

In New York, jury members on duty may not knit.

In Richmond, Virginia restaurants, you may not flip a coin to see who pays for the coffee.

No duck shooting is allowed from a motorboat in Kansas. If you want to hunt ducks, you'll have to row.

An Alabama law says that any kids who play dominoes on Sunday must be fined.

In Nebraska, a person may be arrested for disturbing honey-bees.

New Orleans, Louisiana bans outdoor flower carts.

In New York City during summer, kids may only open fire hydrants that have spray caps.

In Tennessee, the sale of hollow logs has been banned since 1901.

In Chicago, Illinois, you may not sleep under the stars.

Did you know St. Louis has a law against selling fireworks in toy stores?

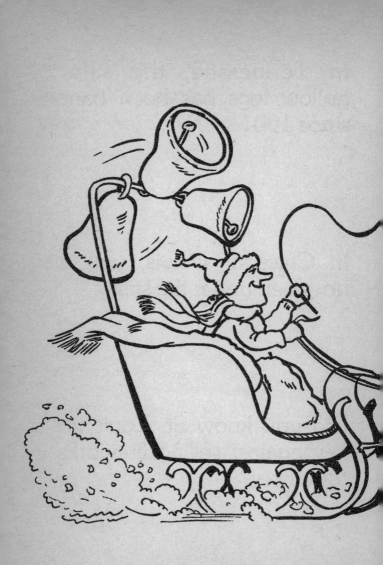

All horse-drawn sleds in Massachusetts must have three bells.

In Seattle, Washington, chickens are not allowed to lay eggs in town.

Climbing trees is against the law in New York City.

In Cleveland, Ohio, teachers must permit small boys to come to school in cowboy boots.

Iowa bans certain words on license plates:

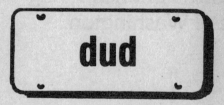

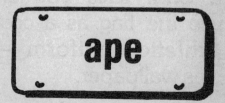

In Michigan, if you carry a flag at a parade, it cannot be red or black.

You may not paint polka dots on the American flag in the state of Washington.

Uncle Sam says you should not use the flag as a costume or athletic uniform — and *never* as wallpaper.

The Governor of Kansas has asked that all homes show the American flag on Mother's Day.

United States law says city lights must be electric — no gaslights!

No one may appear in court barefoot in Hawaii.

And if you drive a car barefoot in New Jersey, you can get in trouble with the law.

In New Jersey, you have to be serious when you pledge to the flag. No jumping up and down, playing a drum, singing a song, or pounding on the table.

You may not tell fortunes for money in Kansas City.

In New York, you are not permitted to throw a ball at someone's head for fun.

Montclair, New Jersey outlaws skateboards.

Disco dance contests lasting more than eight hours are against the law in Tennessee.

It is illegal to feed whiskey or cigarettes to animals at the Manville, New Jersey zoo.

You may not use an elephant to plow a cotton field in North Carolina.

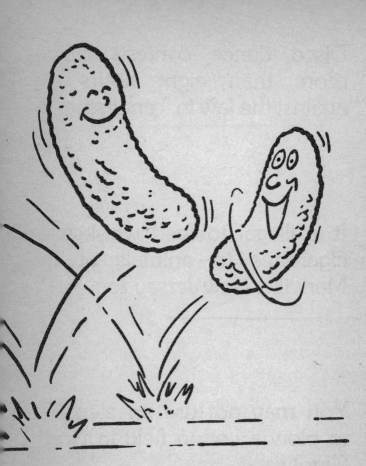

Pickles in Connecticut must bounce.

You may not carry an ice cream cone in your pocket in Lexington, Kentucky.

Watch out for selling ice cream in front of your home if you live in New York. It's against the law. And that goes for frozen yogurt, too!

In Wisconsin, if you buy a meal for 25¢ or more, you are supposed to get free two-thirds of an ounce of famous Wisconsin cheese.

Arlington, Virginia forbids dogs that growl.

Some towns in New Jersey forbid garage sales — unless the house is up for sale.

It is against the law in Tennessee to call another person a coward if he refuses to duel.

In New York City, you may not grow poison ivy or ragweed in your window box.

No bull fighting, says the law in Kentucky.

Dogs and cats in Bessemer, North Carolina are not allowed to fight each other.

In Kansas, it is against the law to keep dead animals in your house.

In Nebraska, tavern owners must have a kettle of soup bubbling.

The law in New Jersey says if you are eating in a restaurant, you may not slurp soup.

You are not permitted to charge for home permanents in Beaumont, Texas.

No bicycle race in New York is supposed to last longer than eight hours.

In Tallahassee, Florida, state inspectors have to smile while conducting automobile safety checks.

Chicago outlaws juggling.

It is against the law in New York to chop down a cherry tree — today, even George Washington would have to have a license.

Ridgewood, New Jersey makes it against the law to build a tree house in your backyard.

In Houston, Texas, boys may not make *goo goo eyes* at girls — there's a *goo goo eyes* law!

Uncle Sam outlaws sound trucks with loud, blaring noises on the streets of Washington, D.C.

Don't let your dog bite the postman. You could be in trouble with the FBI.

In New York, three people are not permitted to ride on a bicycle built for one.

And every bicycle must have a bell.

And you must keep your feet on the pedals, or you'll be in trouble with the law!

It's against the law in Brooklyn, New York to shoot a rabbit from the back of a trolley car.

You must not make cabbage soup on Sunday in Ocean City, New Jersey, unless you cut the cabbage the day before.

San Antonio, Texas does not allow the building of a cotton gin.

You cannot keep snowballs in the refrigerator in Scottsbluff, Nebraska.

In Maine, the first day of winter is Chester Greenwood Day, in honor of the man who invented earmuffs.

No one can *toot-toot* a train whistle in Richmond, Virginia.

In Evansville, Indiana, it is against the law to sell hamburgers on Sunday.

If you have a pet tiger in Louisiana, you must keep him in a cage.

In Willingboro, New Jersey, you may not put a "For Sale" sign in front of your house.

In California, no mean person may force a kid to buy a horror comic book.

In Ohio, it is illegal to gallop your donkey.

In New York, you can be arrested for paying a child under sixteen to collect cigar stumps.

For safety's sake, at wrestling matches in Richmond, Virginia, fans may not buy soda in bottles, only in paper cups.

In Marysville, Ohio, it is against the law to remove the lid of another person's garbage can.

Don't bring a sleigh on to New Jersey highways unless your sleigh bells are ringing.

In Maryland, a woman may not go into her husband's pockets while he is sleeping.

New York State makes it against the law to keep a horse, cow, calf, pig, rabbit, sheep, goat, chicken, duck, or pigeon in your apartment.

(But there's no law against elephants!)

Did you know Fire Island, New York bans the munching of chocolate-chip cookies on the beach?

A child must not have a tattoo in New York.

Maine has very strict fire laws. There is even a law against setting fire to a mule!

In Utah, kids are not permitted to hitch their bicycles
to airplanes.

You may not carry your lunch in a pail on the streets of Riverside, California.

In the state of Washington, chickens are not permitted to live in houses.

Did you know babies in Lynn, Massachusetts are not allowed to drink coffee?

If you see a pigeon fly by carrying mail, don't stop him. It's against the law!

The law in Cleveland says you are allowed to kill your neighbor's chickens if all the other people in the neighborhood give permission.

You must not brush your clothes while traveling on the train in Florida.

The following trades are forbidden in New York City: bone boiling, burning or grinding; the skinning of horses, cows or other animals.

You may not gallop your horse on the boardwalk of Atlantic City.

In Kentucky, you are not allowed to appear on the street in a bathing suit without a policeman standing by.

On New Jersey highways, you may not hitch your horse to a fruit tree.

And in New Jersey towns, you may not hitch your horse to a lamp post or a fire hydrant.

In California, you may not enter a restaurant on horseback.

Suffolk County, Long Island has said *No!* to mobile hot-dog stands — unless a bathroom is *right* nearby.

If you own a restaurant in Birmingham, Alabama, you have to hire someone else to sweep the floor.

If you notice a stray animal in the town of Niagara Falls, tell the town clerk. You'll receive 15¢.

Minneapolis has a lurking ordinance. No person in any public or private place shall lurk.

Restaurant menus in Asotin County, Washington must be in English.

In Tennessee, it has been against the law since 1911 to drop banana peels on the street.

In Virginia, you must not carry a banner for your favorite breakfast cereal.

Kansas law says you should not sell cherry pie on the Sabbath.

You are not allowed to fish for bay scallops in New York on Sunday. (That's their day of rest.)

Pure milk is the only kind the city of Baltimore permits to be sold.

On Sundays in Columbus, Ohio, you are not supposed to buy corn flakes.

In Topeka, Kansas, you may not serve wine in a teacup.

In Mississippi, you may not vote if you have been in a duel.

In San Francisco, it is illegal to use a slug in a parking meter.

No roller skating down the street is allowed in Kansas City, and that goes for sled riding, too.

Salt Lake City says *No!* to people wearing hats with ostrich feathers at public gatherings.

In Berkeley, California, you may not whistle for your escaped canary bird before seven o'clock in the morning!

St. Louis forbids buildings over 35 feet high.

Don't block the sidewalk by playing hopscotch in Griffin, Georgia—or you may hop your way into jail.

If you own more than three dogs in Coon Rapids, Minnesota, you must have a dog kennel license.

In Dunlop, Pennsylvania, if you are found woozy on a horse, the police are supposed to give you a dose of castor oil. (We wonder what they give the horse?)

No horse racing is allowed on the New Jersey Turnpike.

Norfolk, Virginia makes it a crime to keep a messy house.

In Watertown, New York, kids cannot throw snowballs at men wearing top hats.

Richmond limits the number of city pawnshops to twelve.

In Kansas City, barbers must go to their doctors at least once every six months.

Barber poles may not be taller than eight feet in New York City.

It is a crime for a barber to cut hair on Sunday in New Jersey.

If you fall asleep while being shaved by a barber in Erie, Pennsylvania, you can be arrested.

Barbers in Waterloo, Nebraska may not eat onions between 7 a.m. and 7 p.m.

Buffalo herds are not permitted to roam in downtown Denver.

In Pennsylvania, you have to be sixteen years old to get your ears pierced.

A law in Massachusetts forbids putting tomatoes in clam chowder.

Girls have not been allowed to box in New York.

No billboards are allowed at the beach in Southampton, New York.

In Pennsylvania, you must "stop, look and listen" before crossing the railroad tracks.

It's a fact. In Brooklyn, New York, donkeys are not allowed to sleep in bathtubs.

At outdoor concerts in Green, New York, you may not walk backwards on the sidewalk while munching peanuts.

Did you know Smokey the Bear belongs to the United States? No one can use his picture without government permission. And that goes for Woodsy Owl, too, and his slogan, "Give a hoot, don't pollute."